'This is an endearing and helpful book, full of wisdom and insight for Christian parents seeking to make their home a place of love and learning that will bring blessing and delight to their children. It will make you think, and pray!'

Wallace & Lindsay Benn, Speakers who are parents and now grandparents, with over 40 years of ministry experience

'In her inimitable style Ann writes with both beautiful clarity and refreshing, godly challenge. This has been a wonderful spur as we continue to strive to root our family life in the rich soil of the gospel.'

David & Sarah Dargue, parents of three small children and members of Christ Church Newcastle

'In a day where child-led "parenting" is gaining traction, even among Christians, Ann Benton has produced a balanced, biblical and at times humourous corrective which will instill confidence in God's wisdom and design for parenting and fruitful family life.'

Wes & Karen Johnston, serve the church family at Emmanuel Baptist Church, Leeds

'Our culture of hyper-individualism promotes a relentless quest for personal fulfillment. This militates against the formation of households where mutual service draws on and reflects the unfailing love of God. This book offers a refreshing and compelling guide to life in a home where Jesus is Lord. It is firmly grounded in Scripture and reflects the wisdom gained from many years of experience.'

Dr Sharon James, Social Policy Analyst, The Christian Institute

'In The Fruitful Home, *Ann Benton appeals to Psalm 128 as the inspiring basis for raising children in our confused culture. In her thoroughly Biblical and eminently practical way (and with a good dash of English wit), she discusses the foundations on which our homes should be built along with the Gospel-focused furnishings with which to fill them. Parents (and grandparents) will find much encouragement as they seek to honor the Lord in their parenting.'*

Jodi Ware, Southern Seminary faculty wife, member of Seminary Wives Institute faculty

The Fruitful Home

CREATING A GOSPEL CULTURE FOR FAMILY LIFE

Ann Benton

10 Publishing
a division of 10ofthose.com

Copyright © 2019 by Ann Benton

First published in Great Britain in 2019

British Library Cataloguing in Publication Data
A record for this book is available from the British Library

ISBN: 978-1-912373-86-4

Designed and typeset by Pete Barnsley (CreativeHoot.com)

Printed in Denmark by Nørhaven

10Publishing, a division of 10ofthose.com
Unit C, Tomlinson Road, Leyland, PR25 2DY, England

Email: info@10ofthose.com
Website: www.10ofthose.com

1 3 5 7 10 8 6 4 2

Contents

Introduction: What Is a Family?

I have begun to notice how frequently the 'Weekend' sections of Saturday newspapers deal in top tips: '36 ways to keep half-term screen-free'; '17 colourful ideas to spruce up your front garden'; '9 tips on eating more and staying slim'; '23 steps to a perfect night's sleep'; and so forth. Journalists know that we all love a top tip. They are so short, so cheery, so positive and so can-do.

But like the row of shiny new pens in the blazer pocket of the schoolboy sitting his A-level physics, while they may inspire confidence, they are unlikely to materially affect the outcome.

I confess I enjoy top tips myself and read them with immense interest if they are relevant to a current problem I am desperate to solve. And in twenty years of running parenting courses I occasionally dish out my top tips and am touched by how busily the punters scribble them into notebooks. When faced with a parenting conundrum, we would be so delighted to hear of a quick-fix solution. Whether it concerns crying at night, potty-training, sibling rivalry, internet issues or getting children to church, we are ready to try a new strategy, especially if it is presented as effective, fast-acting and convenient.

But even as I hand out my ideas, some of which are based on sound experience, I know that it is not that simple. Raising children (my preferred term for what parents do) does not happen in a vacuum; it happens in a context. And that context is critical. God has given the context for raising children: family.

In the 1970s, when I was starting out on the adventure of motherhood, I came upon a book which recognised the importance of that context. It was called *What Is a Family?* by the writer Edith Schaeffer,[1] wife of the more famous Francis. Recently rereading the book, I was struck by its quirky, intensely personal style. It put me in mind of the kind of grandmother you might meet on a train, who insists on showing you many (too many?) photos of her grandchildren. *What Is a Family?* paints a charming, somewhat bohemian and folksy picture of family life. Yet it had a profound influence upon me and many other Christian mothers of my generation. All over the country, because of her suggestion, mothers began lighting candles at the dinner table to signify the importance of every family meal.

It remains a wise book. Yes, it is a voice from another century and is unsurprisingly dated. Who now, for example, would argue that it is cheaper to make your own clothes than buy them? But beyond all those details *What Is a Family?* remains unique in its insistence on the powerful impact of the rich tapestry that is family life. Where that family life is grounded in Bible truth and a delight in the worship of our loving Creator and Redeemer, a wonderful chemistry is possible. I owe Edith Schaeffer and that book a huge debt.

Instead of seeing parenting as a series of problems to be solved, perhaps we might take a longer and deeper look at the whole of family life, and recognise its pervasive influence. That is the point of this book.

Plants are raised in soil and the nature or quality of that soil is one of the key determining factors of the health of that plant as it grows. Likewise, children are raised in a subculture of family life and according to the health of that subculture they will either wither or flourish.

Let's think about that reality. Let's talk about the soil of family life. The answer to how to parent lies there.

1

A Happy House

When my sisters and I were children, one of the storybooks we had in our comparatively small collection at home was a clothbound book (A4 size) published in 1946 with attractive coloured pictures. It was *The Children of Happy House* by Enid Blyton. This is the story of a family who moved to a new house in the country, and is a charming evocation of a secure family life where nothing more alarming happens than the breaking of glass in the next-door neighbour's cucumber frame. Written at a time when Britain was just emerging from the uncertainty, loss and fear of invasion of World War Two, it was no doubt a sweet diversion, expressing hopes for a better life for the nation's children. I recall it now with some nostalgia.

Such twee fodder would doubtless go into the bin of any self-respecting, twenty-first-century publisher of children's books. They like – in the name of reality – dysfunction, attitude and flawed, vulnerable characters. They may have a point; I am not defending *The Children of Happy House* as great literature. But the Bible has its own 'happy house', a freeze-frame of a delightful and fruitful family life. It is found in Psalm 128:

Blessed are all who fear the Lord,
*   who walk in obedience to him.*
You will eat the fruit of your labour;
*   blessings and prosperity will be yours.*
Your wife will be like a fruitful vine
*   within your house;*
your children will be like olive shoots
*   round your table.*
Yes, this will be the blessing
*   for the man who fears the Lord.*
May the Lord bless you from Zion;
*   may you see the prosperity of Jerusalem*
*   all the days of your life.*
May you live to see your children's children –
*   peace be on Israel.*

Psalm 128 does not major on dysfunction, attitude and weakness – although there is plenty of that in the Bible. It presents a happy house indeed: a house of security, order, peace, prosperity and beauty. It depicts a harmonious family seated around a table, perhaps from three generations of God-fearing people. The end of the psalm shows that the blessing spreads outwards to God's people and to the wider community – like widening circles in a lake when a stone is thrown.

Is the Bible unreal to give us this picture? Is it the Christian equivalent of an idealistic picture on the Corn Flakes packet? Of course not! This psalm, one of the psalms of ascent or journeying psalms, is a call to obedience and faith – at home. It is both aspirational and inspirational. It is showing us what could and should happen in the believer's home. And the necessary condition is fear of the Lord. Healthy family life starts with worshipping the Lord.

To fear the Lord – that is, to recognise in your very soul the presence, awesome power and matchless grace of the transcendent, personal, triune God – means that you will love him and want to walk in his ways. And when you live like that, you will create around you a subculture of family life, a subculture which is Christian and distinctively so. This is the soil in which to grow healthy, rounded human beings.

One of Edith Schaeffer's many definitions of the family is 'an ecologically balanced environment for the growth of human beings'. This is the way it is intended to be. God did not first make children and let them grow up in the garden untended, as it were. He made the grown-ups first and then he gave them babies.

Psalm 128 pictures a whole family subculture in one frame – this will be further unpacked in the following chapter. Without this foundation, even the best techniques and top tips will be insufficient and probably fruitless in creating a happy house.

This is a critical point in our current secular, atheistic age. Parents, grandparents and churches – who have a heartfelt and right desire to see the next generation won for Christ – need to recognise the atmosphere of the age. Its values, priorities, ambitions and glories are ever present in the air we breathe *and have invaded our homes.* I shall term this the prevailing culture. Its impact on us all is far greater than we realise. It is subtle; it is generally invisible; it is frequently very attractive; and it is immensely powerful.

Every family, consciously or unconsciously, creates its own subculture. Very often, and quite naturally, it draws from the prevailing culture in doing so. Even the names you chose for your children reflect the age you live in. My husband and I thought we were being terrifically original (and proudly biblical) when we chose the name Matthew for our firstborn. We knew no other children of that name. It was only later we discovered that it was one of the most common names of his generation. How did that happen? Answer: it must have been in the ether.

We are so much more influenced by the prevailing winds of fashion and culture than we care to admit – from the colour we paint a baby's bedroom, to the books we read and the music we listen to; from the things we talk about over dinner to the way we spend our money and our time. Our prevailing culture is a package and it carries its own message. Much may be harmless but plenty is not.

Schools, in a competitive marketplace, recognise the importance of ethos. Just visit a few of their websites and you will notice the emphasis that is placed on ethos in selling a school. One prestigious school in my neighbourhood markets itself thus:

You will always be curious
You will always value others
You will always believe in being yourself
You will always have a life less ordinary
You will always be a community within
    the community
You will always want to make a difference …

Now will there be explicit lessons on those subjects? Probably not. But those messages will intentionally be there in the warp and woof of school life. Schools have their own subculture. Traditions will be in place; mottos will be repeated; attitudes will be discouraged; habits will be formed.

However, having been a teacher, I am all too aware that the impact school has on a child is minimal compared to that of home. Home wins. So here is the question: what will your child always be as a result of growing up in your home? Always ambitious? Always feeling a failure? Always arrogant? Always able to take correction? Always materialistic? Always generous? You get the point.

Paul McCartney wrote the song 'Let It Be' recalling his mother. She died when he was only in his teens. And yet something of what she was and taught him stayed with him. According to the song, it sustained him in a dark place for many years after her death: 'And when the night is cloudy there is still a light that shines on me, speaking words of wisdom ... '

Naturally the ethos of most families is undergirded by love. That is taken as a given in this book and indeed in Psalm 128. It is undisputed that the unconditional love that parents give their children, especially in their earliest years, is a critical factor for healthy development. This too is imaging the God who made us.

But human love can be blind, as we know. Love can overlook what it should see. Love can be distracted and not realise the soil, the ethos, that is being unconsciously engendered.

Psalm 128 would not agree that with the Beatles that 'all you need is love'. It argues that all you need is parents who fear the Lord and walk in obedience to him.

Family subculture, ethos, soil – for good or ill – has a telling and lasting effect. If the family subculture is sound, parents will muddle through the stresses and strains of potty-training, sibling rivalries and teenage angst, with or without a how-to guide, and still come out smiling.

Psalm 128 is a foundational aspiration for all believing parents, calling them to continually fear the Lord and walk in his ways. Such a stance and direction will be, as they say, a 'game changer'. And not only will the children in those families thrive, but the blessing will spread outwards to church and nation.

PART A

Foundations: Building the House

If you want to build a ship, don't drum up people to collect wood and don't assign them tasks and work, but rather teach them to long for the endless immensity of the sea.

(From *The Wisdom of the Sands* by Antoine de Saint-Exupéry)[2]

2

A House of Structure

Something there is that doesn't love a wall …

(From 'Mending Wall' by Robert Frost)[3]

The first three aspects of a happy house are foundational, but the notion of structure is the one most challenged by the prevailing culture. The poet Robert Frost observed his all too frequent wall-mending activities were due to the corrosion and damage perpetrated by weather and beasts. The same observation about the need for incessant repairs could be made about all the boundaries and structures of family life. These went unchallenged in the Western world for centuries, but are now so disliked and, where possible, dismantled – by broadcasters, politicians, celebrities, tweeters and bloggers who want to be thought cool.

But a happy house is unashamed of its structures. Three are implicitly celebrated in Psalm 128.

1. Marriage

Your wife will be like a fruitful vine
within your house.

(Psalm 128:3)

The picture in Psalm 128 is of a man, his wife and their children. The wife is a fruitful vine, flourishing under her husband's care and protection. He is proud of her.

Even one generation ago one might not have felt it necessary to draw attention to this, but it is clear that a biblical family is headed up by a man and a woman who are married to each other. That is the first aspect of the structure. The psalm points to a man's labour in providing for the family and the wife's fruitful, nurturant qualities. This is not to denigrate or veto female salaried employment, which can be both necessary and useful. Nevertheless, the male/female distinctives indicated here are the particular duties of husband and wife, father and mother. God made humankind two ways, male and female, who are equal but distinct.

We find a counter example in Proverbs:

Under three things the earth trembles,
*   under four it cannot bear up:*
a servant who becomes king,
*   a godless fool who gets plenty to eat,*
a contemptible woman who gets married,
and a servant who displaces her mistress.

(Proverbs 30:21–23)

Many Bible commentators believe that where Proverbs contains a numerical set (x and x+1, as in this case) it is the last, additional item of the set that provides the key. The maidservant who displaces her mistress is suggestive of an illicit, adulterous relationship. Where that boundary is crossed, other symptoms of dysfunction appear: authority is undermined (with the servant taking over); discipline is abandoned (with the lazy member of the household happily feeding his face, taking not giving); and there is deep unhappiness at the very heart of the home (with an unloved wife). That is why 'the earth trembles'. Dysfunction spells disaster. Abandon God's structures at your peril. The Western world is only just beginning to reap the harvest it has sown.

But a Christian family has every reason to celebrate marriage. Build that into your routines. As wedding anniversaries come and go, overtly recognise the stability that the shared history brings. In these days of keeping photos on phones, perhaps there is still a place for the album you can get down from its shelf and pour over with your children, saying, 'This is us.' Use marriage words like: wife, husband, mother, father – though some would like to erase them from the dictionary. Draw attention to the beauty of heterosexual marriage, one of God's great ideas with significance beyond your own four walls (see Ephesians 5:22–33).

Children need to see a happy marriage lived out. Sadly, evangelicals have sometimes been reticent in this regard. In Anthony Trollope's novel *Rachel Ray* there is this description of a supposedly evangelical attitude to marriage:

Men and women, according to her theory, were right to marry and have children; but she thought that such marriages should be contracted not only in a solemn spirit, but with a certain dinginess of solemnity, with a painstaking absence of mirth, that would divest love of its worldly alloy.[4]

What a travesty! Christians are right to take marriage seriously, but there should never be a dingy solemnity about Christian marriage. Having argued against the legal redefinition of marriage in the earlier years of this century, we must be careful not to redefine marriage in our homes by letting them become dull and mirthless. Rather let us prove we believe in marriage by investing in and enjoying extremely good ones. As David Gibson writes in his commentary on Ecclesiastes 9:7–10:

'Enjoy life with your spouse whom you love'. Cherish and protect the person God has given

you. If you're married, don't downplay this. We are not told: live with your wife, or put up with your wife, but rather, enjoy life with your wife.[5]

In our churches of course we don't want to make single people feel lesser beings; they are not. Singleness is good and useful. But marriage is good too. While teaching our children to find contentment in the state God ordains for us, it is not wrong to raise our children to aspire to be at some point married. And of course marriage is the only proper context for sex. So our children need to see their parents, appropriately of course (and not to make them cringe), demonstrating affectionate tenderness towards each other.

Nor is this section of the book intended to make single parents feel bad. Most single parents I meet are all too well aware that what they have is not ideal. Raising a child is very hard work on your own. It can be done and done well, but it is tough because it was not designed to be that way. We do those brave single parents and their children no favours when we deny this.

We also need to make sure our children understand the difference between marriage and a wedding. One of the saddest evidences of the deconstruction of marriage is the fact that the reason couples now give for why they don't marry is that they can't afford a wedding. And when they do marry, the focus is all about the wedding day, which has to compete in its novelty and style with others that have gone before. It is estimated that the wedding industry generates 49–51 billion dollars annually. I was delighted to hear recently of a Christian couple who got married during a 'normal' Sunday morning service at church, then enjoyed tea and cake with everyone afterwards. And why not? In bigging up marriage to our children, let us be careful to avoid the worldly and frankly commercial propagation of the romantic wedding dream. Talk to them more about the beauty of the long-term marriage promises: 'for better, for worse, for richer, for poorer, in sickness and in health'.

2. Authority

It is clear in Psalm 128 that there is a head of the house and beside him a wife, and that children are under their care and authority. Mothers and fathers have benign authority over their children:

not waving a big stick, but lovingly teaching their children to respect and obey them because that is right (Ephesians 6:1); it pleases the Lord (Colossians 3:20). Note as well that while the fifth commandment says, 'Honour your father and your mother' (summarising God's pattern for authority and how children are to be raised), Leviticus 19:3 says, 'Each of you must respect your mother and father'. That inversion makes clear that a mother and father speak as one. No mother needs to respond, 'Wait till your father gets home.' Nor is respect for, and obedience to, parents a vain hope or an abuse of children's rights. It is to be an absolute expectation in which children are consistently trained. Set boundaries. Say no. Follow through in your discipline. Be consistent. This is for the safety, health and happiness of your child, the peace and harmony of your home, the good of the whole community, and your own sanity and joy:

> *Discipline your children, and they will give*
> *you peace;*
> *they will bring you the delights you desire.*
>
> (Proverbs 29:17)

Proverbs 28 and 29 have a good deal to say about this use, or abuse, of authority, whether in a nation, community or home. Similar principles apply in each case.

> *When a country is rebellious, it has many rulers,*
> *but a ruler with discernment and*
> *knowledge maintains order.*
>
> (Proverbs 28:2)

So within a home there should be one source of authority, not many. Children need to know who is in charge. Mayhem at home means the system has broken down. What is required is understanding and knowledge that the basis of law and justice is outside themselves. This is not oppression.

> *Evildoers do not understand what is right,*
> *but those who seek the LORD understand*
> *it fully.*
>
> (Proverbs 28:5)

Parental authority is derived authority, as the man who fears the Lord very well knows.

3. Routines

Note what the family are doing in Psalm 128: they are sitting around a table eating together. This is not just about the food – in fact, you could argue that the menu is the least important aspect. Instead, it is the very epitome of family belonging, the essence of togetherness and the means of face-to-face communication.

Eating together is just one, although among the most important, of the many routines you will weave into your family life. Routines express who you are and what you think is important. They are also excellent for discipline as they communicate an unspoken expectation about how, when and where things will be done.

In a happy house, where the head of the house fears the Lord and loves to walk in his ways, there will be other routines and traditions as well. The family in Psalm 128 is longing for the prosperity of Jerusalem (verse 5). This sets the orientation of the man. His family therefore know where they are going, and the rhythms and routines of their collective lives will reflect that orientation.

For the Christian family today priorities are shaped by the overarching purpose to glorify

God by a concern for his kingdom. This is the big vision which guides and governs everything. The rhythms and routines of our lives will be gateways to that vision. There are cues and expectations, mostly unspoken, every step of the way.

So, for example, there will be those traditions that follow the seasons and the pattern of the Christian year. These you will own by inventing and including little things that are exclusive to your family. Children love traditions. In fact, it is quite hard to stop them making them. Repeat an event just once and they will think of it as a tradition. A family of my acquaintance took their holidays at the same farmhouse in North Wales for many years. Now, when they revisit with their grown children, they are still obliged to visit every one of the old haunts. Turn that love of tradition to your family's good. Use repeated experiences, mottos and activities – big and small – to identify who you are, what you stand for and where you are going.

Equally, kingdom priorities will dictate some of the daily and weekly routines in a happy house: the assembling of God's people on

Sundays, prayer and the reading of Scripture. These have massive significance for a happy house, as we shall see in later chapters.

But the Lord's Day must have a special significance, because so much is made of it in Scripture. This is a routine established by God – the one day in seven set apart for him. And you can mark it not merely by meeting with your church family but by the small traditions: the kind of food you eat, the music you listen to, the stories you tell, the guests you receive and even the clothes you wear. In this last respect I am not arguing for showing off fine and fancy 'Sunday-best' clothes, but simply saying that the ritual of choosing particular clothes for a particular occasion carries a message. It has become very fashionable to dress down for church, in reaction against this old Sunday-best idea. Of course it is true that God looks on the heart, so there is a sense in which God is not interested in our clothes. But the fact is that our hearts are to some extent moulded by our habits and routines. So a careless approach to dress might, to a developing heart and mind, be translated to a careless approach to the Lord himself.

Although the Christian faith contains a message, and a crucially important one, we should perhaps beware of *reducing* it to a message. Let it come through in the rhythms of your family life. These rhythms and routines will be about what, or whom, you love.

A happy house, then, is a house of structure. Some things should be immovable. All those warnings in the Old Testament about not moving an ancient boundary stone (see, for example, Proverbs 22:28) perhaps have a metaphorical meaning beyond the division of the Promised Land. God has given us precious boundaries for our health and happiness: marriage, the authority of parents over children and setting aside one day in seven for God. Each of these three has been savagely attacked by the prevailing culture in the last few decades. But the Christian family not only keeps them intact, but displays them to the glory of God.

3

A House of Substance

Then, while Rat busied himself fetching plates, and knives and forks, and mustard which he mixed up in an egg-cup, the Mole, his bosom still heaving with the stress of his recent emotion, related – somewhat shyly at first, but with more freedom as he warmed to his subject – how this was planned and how that was thought out, and how this was got through a windfall from an aunt, and that was a wonderful find and a bargain and this other thing was bought out of laborious savings and a certain amount of 'going without'.

(From *The Wind in the Willows*
by Kenneth Grahame)[6]

The first time we visit the house of a friend or a stranger we quite naturally observe what they have on their walls, on their shelves and in their rooms. This is not, one would hope, to judge, but because we are curious. Just as in Mole's case, there may well be a story attached to each item.

Proverbs acknowledges this:

By wisdom a house is built,
and through understanding it is established;
through knowledge its rooms are filled
with rare and beautiful treasures.

(Proverbs 24:3–4)

So look around your house. What fills it?

We fill our houses with stuff; we fill our children's bedrooms with stuff. A survey in 2011 estimated there was 7.3 billion pounds worth of paraphernalia in children's bedrooms. Are these the rare and beautiful treasures that wisdom accumulates? I doubt it. What will really enhance their lives? Evidently we need to look beyond material possessions.

Listen, my son, to your father's instruction
  and do not forsake your mother's teaching.
They are a garland to grace your head
  and a chain to adorn your neck.

(Proverbs 1:8–9)

Teaching the wisdom of Scripture is what will beautify your children and furnish your house. So instructing your children in biblical truth should be the central feature of your input. Give time and attention to how, where and when you will do this.

Digestible food

You do not start a baby on solid food by giving him a plate of steak and chips. Apart from being edible, food should be digestible. And so should truth when it is served up to children.

There is a searing indictment of a Christian upbringing in the autobiographical work *Father and Son* by Edmund Gosse.[7] Gosse was the son of a nineteenth-century naturalist who was also a leading light in his local Brethren assembly. Gosse writes bitterly of his childhood and his father's sincere but ill-advised methods, commenting that 'he was in a tremendous hurry to push on my spiritual growth, and he fed me with theological meat it was impossible for me to digest'.

He recalls too that he knew of (and envied) other evangelical children of his generation who were brought up on a work called 'Line upon line: here a little and there a little'. This was evidently a more gentle and fitting resource for the instruction of children. That no such approach was used for Gosse as a boy turned out to be a tragic error; he later rejected his parents' deep and sincerely held Christian convictions. Gosse himself describes his parents' method as 'building spires and battlements without taking pains to settle a foundation'.

So as parents we need to think about age-appropriate content.

Nourishing content

On the other hand, in our concerns for digestion, we might be inclined not to feed our children anything substantial. Sadly, many bespoke Bible stories for children have been therapeutically modified to empty them of any doctrinal substance. You may, for example, find many a children's book on Noah on the shelves of your local bookshop, but few of them will mention the fact that the flood was God's judgment on a wicked world.

So discernment is needed. You need to sort out the solid stuff from the twaddle. Good and beautifully presented Bible story books for children are out there. Take time to check out what is available. But think bigger than Bible stories. Think of Bible overviews, theology, church history and church governance. You want your children to be wise for salvation so teach them the gospel. Make it your relentless quest to resource Bible time with materials that are faithful to Scripture as well as engaging.

An appetising meal

It is so sad if family Bible time becomes boring and an occasion when the children zone out and switch off. Sometimes you have to be inventive. If you can't buy materials to teach your children truth in a winsome, winning way, then make your own. That process will bless you as much as it blesses them.

It was on account of this – a lack of materials which taught Bible truth at a level my children could understand and enjoy – that I invented my own story for our children. In our toybox lurked: a cheap, plastic clockwork train; a wooden horse on wheels; a hand-knitted soldier; and a rather ghastly stuffed toy with a big grin. These became the dramatis personae of a story I devised and taught at the breakfast table day by day to help our children understand and learn a young child's version of the shorter catechism.[8] I did the same with the Ten Commandments and the Lord's Prayer.[9]

Perhaps you could get creative and do something similar yourself. This may well seem daunting, but the main thing is to teach your children something of substance. Ground them in the gospel. Teach them about what church is and what it is for. And make the experience as enjoyable as it is instructive.

Memorable truth

From earliest times Christians have catechised their children, that is, taught them in question and answer form all the basic tenets of Christian truth. When all kinds of rote learning were ditched in the educational fashions of the later twentieth century, this practice fell into disrepute.

For a happy house, a house of substance, let's revive the habit of rote learning, whether that is a catechism, a creed, a prayer or Scripture verses. Sometimes these things can be set to music, an excellent aide-memoire; sometimes you can invent accompanying sign language. And all the family should rise to the challenge. This one is not just for the children, although they may well turn out to be better at it than you are. Make it a fun family routine.

Learning by heart is commended in Scripture as a training not so much of memory but in godly habits:

> *Pay attention and turn your ear to the sayings*
> *of the wise;*
> *apply your heart to what I teach,*
> *for it is pleasing when you keep them in your heart*
> *and have all of them ready on your lips.*
> *So that your trust may be in the LORD …*

> (Proverbs 22:17–19)

Note that the sayings are kept in the heart. In Bible terms this is not the seat of the emotions, but the place where thought, will and desire resides. Learning by heart will not leave the heart untouched, although it might appear somewhat mechanical. Words that go in and lie dormant in the recesses of mind may be slow burners but may yet accomplish significant work.

Living it out

Understand also, though, that Christianity is a message that must be lived. There is serious warning in these words by James K.A. Smith:

> You could have Bible 'inputs' every day and yet still have a household whose frantic rhythms are humming along with the consumerist myth of production and consumption. You might have Bible verses on the wall of every room of the house and yet the unspoken rituals reinforce self-centredness rather than sacrifice.[10]

In contrast, Paul's words to Timothy refer to the profound impact of his mother and grandmother:

I am reminded of your sincere faith, which first lived in your grandmother Lois and in your mother Eunice and, I am persuaded, now lives in you also.

(2 Timothy 1:5)

Here the faith lived. There was a verbal message, which made the young Timothy wise for salvation. However, it impacted him not just because he had learned it and knew it, but because he knew those from whom he learned it (2 Timothy 3:14–15) and how it transformed them.

Bible reading and prayer are not just things we do but things that do something to us. Their substance has the power to fill a happy house with rare and wonderful treasures.

Part of the furniture

Bible truth leads to such a house when those who have known it best and longest really enjoy it. It will frequently invade conversations. Considered permanently relevant, it permeates the whole day, every day. It refuses to be kept in its box, but informs every attitude and action, generally quite unconsciously.

In the first few chapters of Numbers Moses instructs the Israelites how to arrange their campsite. It is a significant routine, always placing the tabernacle at the centre of things as a permanent reminder of the centrality of God, his word and his sacrifices. Our routines of Bible teaching must also carry that message that God is at the centre, not us. Likewise, just as the Israelites had to wait for the pillar of fire or cloud to move before they did, so a Christian family can learn by the practice of prayer that we dare not take a step without God's permission and aid.

Making sense of the world

My original edition of Enid Blyton's *The Children of Happy House* had beautifully drawn endpapers which as a child I pored over as much as the stories themselves. The endpapers were a pictorial map of the village in which Happy House was situated. And the map had legends, like 'where the old man gave Jane a penny to get home', so that the stories were referenced. As I read or thought about them, I could trace Jane's journey home with my finger.

Grounding our children in gospel truth and a Bible worldview is that kind of a map. It is our reference point so that what we do at home relates to the whole universe. It is our orientation, keeping us true to what actually is. For the Christian faith stands on objective truth. This is no postmodern nonsense that validates whatever is 'true for you'. It is not our adherence to the Christian faith that makes it true, but rather the fact that it is true means that we will live in it and walk in it, or neglect it at our peril. The objective truth may be sometimes inconvenient and uncomfortable, but it is not going to go away.

Psalm 36 contrasts an ungodly and a godly subculture. The man who does not fear the Lord has a high view of himself; no sense of sin; no wisdom; no moral compass. But the man who knows the Lord declares:

For with you is the fountain of life;
in your light we see light.

(Psalm 36:9)

Such a man has found refuge in the shadow of God's wings; he has been well fed; his hunger and thirst have been more than satisfied by the abundance of God's house. He is thoroughly enraptured. And so he becomes enlightened. His whole perspective is corrected. Mothers and fathers who recognise how priceless God's unfailing love is will help their children also to see the world through the true lens of God's word. That is treasure indeed.

The prevailing culture is typically very shallow. But a Christian family life, where Bible truth is loved and lived, is a house of substance. Its rooms are being filled with rare and beautiful treasures – some, like Mole's precious possessions, fall into their lap as a matter of heritage, but others are gained at some cost.

Come, my children, listen to me;
I will teach you the fear of the Lord.

(Psalm 34:11)

4

A House of Story

'Is it a 'tory?' asked Stephen, coming up beside his father's chair.

'You bet your life it is a story, a crackerjack of a story.'

'Tell it to me,' said Stephen. He leaned both elbows on the arm of the chair, put his round chin on his hands, tipped his head to one side and turned his shining dark eyes up toward his father's face.

(From *The Home-maker* by Dorothy Canfield Fisher)[11]

In 1841 crowds stormed the New York docks. They wanted news. Was it about the latest Afghan war? Was it about prices in the tea trade? No and no. The question that was on everyone's lips that day was 'Does little Nelly live?' They were referring to the plight of little Nell, the child heroine of Charles Dickens' novel *The Old Curiosity Shop*. Because that story was serialised and released in instalments, readers had been left with a cliffhanger regarding the ailing child. It had seemed like a long wait for the next issue. They were as desperate to know the news on Little Nell as if she were a real member of their family. But it was a mere fiction, though the story had captured the hearts of the reading public.

We are story-making and story-telling creatures. That is how God made us. People are captured by stories, as is repeatedly evidenced by those we know who are desperate not to miss the next episode of *The Archers*, *EastEnders*, *Peter Kay's Car Share* or whatever else everyone is talking about. We are made for stories.

Stories capture our hearts. In the previous chapter we talked about the importance of truth going into our hearts, shaping us and how we think about the world and our own lives. The power of story teaches us that this is the key to our heart transformation.

The story of your life

We look on our own lives as stories. Our fascination with genealogy and the popularity of TV programmes such as *Who Do You Think You Are?* betrays a sense of our significance, and which makes no sense within an evolutionary worldview.

Children have questions about their own story: 'Where did I come from? Who am I?' These are questions which a good grounding in Scripture will answer. But there is more to discover. What story will you live by? The Bible's answer is the gospel. So you should guide your children in an understanding of God's big story.

I don't just mean here the essence of John 3:16 – that is, that Jesus died so that we might have eternal life – though of course this is a crucial part of it. Rather, as your children explore the world, teach them to admire what God has so lovingly and intricately made. When they see the ugliness caused by sin, including their own, teach them its source in the Fall. Be unafraid to acknowledge suffering and the bewilderment it brings. There are questions about this we cannot answer, but we can look at the cross and see how Jesus suffered for a rebellious human race. Teach them to recognise God's mercies with every meal and song. Teach them that life is a gift, but not to be squandered. Teach them that we must all give account of our lives to God. All these things come into his big story.

The book of Joel gives an example of this:

Tell it to your children,
and let your children tell it to their children,
and their children to the next generation.

(Joel 1:3)

What was the story they were to tell? It was the story of an invasion of locusts and the devastation it caused. This is a story of God dealing with his people in judgment, but it is also a story of hope. It teaches about living with consequences, about learning from mistakes, about repentance and the process of change.

Testimony

Proverbs has another example:

For I too was a son to my father,
still tender, and cherished by my mother.

Then he taught me, and said to me,
 'Take hold of my words with all your heart …
(Proverbs 4:3–4)

In this case it seems the father is telling of his own journey to faith: his testimony. That is a story, different in each case, which each of us should tell our children. Do your children know how and why you believed? As I write this, I have recently marked the fiftieth anniversary of my own coming to faith. I am in the process of making a picture book about that event which I intend to share with our grandchildren when we spend time with them in the summer holidays. I want to tell my story because stories have an unconscious dynamic which brings truth to life. That is one of the reasons why stories capture hearts. Stories also linger in the imagination. Stories convey not merely truth but love.

So tell your children stories, eyeball to eyeball. Capture them with God's big story, but also with your own little story which is part of that big story.

Deuteronomy 6 pictures a time after the exodus when a child might ask his parents, 'Why do we actually do this – bother with the law, bring sacrifices, keep the Passover, and so on?' Moses says this is a parent's opportunity to tell the story of what parents had seen and experienced: the story of God's amazing rescue. A present-day teenager might ask a similar kind of question, possibly in a hostile way: 'What's the point of all this?' Here is your opportunity to tell the story. You have, or should have, a reason for the rituals which are your life.

For example, maybe a teenager complains, 'Why do we go to church every Sunday?'

Your response could be: 'Because it's a way we acknowledge that this is God's world, not ours.'

In addition, pray together regularly. That is a powerful way to acknowledge dependency on a sovereign, loving God. Thoroughly involve yourself in the community of God's people – your local church – not just being there but being *all* there. Have rituals and traditions which explore and celebrate the story you live by, perhaps attached to Christmas and Easter, or the seasons, or church events or camps.

Helpful fiction

But don't forget other stories too. When Edmund Gosse was being raised in a strict Calvinistic home in the nineteenth century, one of his chief resentments was story deprivation:

> Never in all my early childhood, did anyone address to me the affecting preamble, 'Once upon a time!' I was told about missionaries but never about pirates; I was familiar with humming-birds but I had never heard of fairies. Jack the Giant-Killer, Rumpelstiltskin and Robin Hood were not of my acquaintance, and though I understood about wolves, Little Red Riding Hood was a stranger even by name.[12]

Gosse concedes that in excluding imaginary books and supplying only those with facts, his parents were merely attempting to make him truthful. But it left him sceptical and itching to leave their traditions. He says that 'the soft folds of supernatural fancy' would have made him more content to rest in those traditions. However ignoring a child's imagination is done, it crushes something that makes us human. And as

C.S. Lewis often remarked, truth can frequently find a better vehicle in a work of fantasy (like *The Chronicles of Narnia*) than something which purports to be realistic.

Since the invention of the printing press, countless stories have been written. All the best ones are redemption stories. Teach your children to find the themes of God's big story in these smaller stories. While it may seem more obvious how you can do that with Lewis's Narnian adventures, nearly all stories of any worth carry themes to ponder, examples to follow, errors to avoid and rescues to take our breath away or move our hearts. Any story in which evil is finally destroyed and good triumphs echoes the Bible. Any story which shows the misery of sin confirms Genesis 3. So furnish your children with stories which echo the big story.

Quality writing

I believe it was C.S. Lewis who said that a children's story that can only be enjoyed by children is not a good children's story. That seems a very useful guide to the selection of children's reading materials.

This whole theme is explored brilliantly in the book *Honey for a Child's Heart* by Gladys Hunt.[13] She says, 'Words fitly spoken, characters memorable, a theme to challenge the heart – this is what we want for our children!' She gives many useful suggestions and ideas for a diet of good reading, explaining, 'Reading should offer the solace of hope and goodness, of another world where truth and right triumph.'

Such criteria are certainly true of John Bunyan's *Pilgrim's Progress*,[14] surely a must-read for any Christian home, although perhaps not in its original language. Having said that, many generations of children were brought up on and loved the original.

More reading time, fewer screens

Reading out loud with your children is a shared adventure to be pursued way beyond their ability to read for themselves. Watching a film together can have a similar power and supply fuel for much discussion, thought and mirth. But such family film times, fun as we found them to be, should never replace verbal story-telling or story-reading. Screens do not have the power to capture the imagination in the same way that purely verbal stories do. A story visually presented on a screen forces the film-maker's imagination on us, but words leave us free to imagine.

Creating a world with words alone is a peculiarly engaging activity, but an appetite for it will only be engendered by regular, delightful doses. If stories of various styles and lengths are to be incorporated into the rhythms of a busy family life, the parents will have to make time for them in increasingly crowded schedules. Screens, whether they are phones, tablets or television, fill our lives and divert our gaze. They tend also to be addictive. However, if you combine that story-telling activity with a cuddle, the smell of soap and shampoo following a bath and a sense of genuine shared anticipation, you have the recipe for the kind of fantastic routine your children will never want you to stop.

I began this chapter with a quotation from *The Home-maker* by Dorothy Canfield Fisher. This is a story of a woman who was famous for being a wonderful housewife, but thinks that is about having a spotless kitchen floor and spotless children's faces. She works and slaves and is permanently resentful while her children are cowed, angry and miserable. Then, one day, her husband has an accident and can no longer go out to work. He becomes the true home-maker as, rising from the depression brought on by his own sense of failure as a father, he discovers the power of story and his deprived children begin to live and love and laugh.

The story that begins this transformation is Bunyan's. It captivates their neglected, naughty little boy and the troubled, discouraged father as he tells it. It becomes part of their story. As Dorothy writes:

The words rang in Stephen's ears. He said them over to himself in a murmur as he handled his top absently. 'All the twumpets sounded. All the twumpets sounded on the other side.'

After a time he asked, 'Father, what's a twumpet?'

A question from Stephen!

His father turned his head from the frying-pan from which the bacon sent up its thin blue wreaths of smoke. 'What's a trumpet? It's a great, gleaming brass horn which always, always has been blown where there has been a victory – like this!' He flung up his arm, holding an imaginary trumpet to his lips, 'Taranta! Taranta!' He sounded it out ringingly! That's the way they sounded when Mr. Valiant crossed the Dark River.'

'Taranta!' murmured Stephen to himself. 'And all the twumpets sounded.'

He sat in the sun on the kitchen floor, looking up at his crippled father frying bacon. For both of them the kitchen was ringing with the bright, brazen shout of victory.

A happy house harnesses the power of story.

PART B

Furnishings: Living the Story

We can't counter the power of cultural liturgies with didactic information poured into our intellects. We can't recalibrate the heart from the top down through merely informational measures. The orientation of our heart happens from the bottom up, through the formation of our habits of desire.

(From *You Are What You Love* by James K.A. Smith)

5

A House of Sorrow

He had meant them to be good, but his cares had been directed to the understanding and the manners, not the disposition; and of the necessity of self-denial and humility, he feared they had never heard from any lips that could profit them.

(From *Mansfield Park* by Jane Austen)[15]

When Sir Thomas Bertram of Mansfield Park reviews the way he has parented the wayward Maria and Julia, he has much cause for regret. Something must have been wanting, he concludes: 'They had been instructed theoretically in their religion, but never required to bring it into daily practice.' In particular the gushing flattery of their aunt Mrs Norris, and his own attempts to counter that by extreme strictness and coldness, had worked only to drive them back to Aunt Norris, whose blindness of affection had led her to excess and unwarranted praise in every situation.

In a Christian home, gospel themes (such as recognition of sin, grace, forgiveness, service and a desire for God's glory) will be seen in the patterns of life. These routines and rituals are part of a script we follow that shapes our choices, attitudes and behaviour. As I explain the ways in which such a happy house will live, it may surprise readers that I start with the subject of sorrow. But to live the story means to be acquainted with grief. We follow and love a Saviour who was a man of sorrows, and this should emerge in our daily practices.

Reason to cry

There are legitimate times for being sad. Indeed, when babies come into the world, more or less the first thing they do apart from breathe is cry. As the shorter catechism reminds us, all mankind was born into a state of sin and misery. At the risk of being accused of giving way to a doom-and-gloom scenario, I believe the Bible gives us good reason to recognise this in various ways. Take this instruction to the women of Jerusalem:

> *Now, you women, hear the word of the LORD;*
> *open your ears to the words of his mouth.*
> *Teach your daughters how to wail;*
> *teach one another a lament.*

(Jeremiah 9:20)

The context here is the prophesied destruction of Jerusalem by the Babylonians – under the ferocious Nebuchadnezzar in the sixth century BC. The denounced priests and false prophets said, 'Peace, peace … where there is no peace' (Jeremiah 6:14). In contrast, Jeremiah effectively said in 9:20, 'Wake up to the real situation. There is something here worth crying about.'

We might like to paint a facade over our family lives which says everything is always wonderful, but there is not warrant for that in the Bible. The inhabitants of a happy house know how to weep. There are things that should, rightly, make us sorrowful.

Appropriate use of praise

One of the improvements in parenting styles over the last twenty years has been the recognition that children need encouragement. Praise and encouragement are really crucial tools in managing behaviour. However, this concept is now so firmly ingrained in the popular mind that it has a tendency to lead to a continuous stream of affirmation from parental lips, whether deserved or not – like the example of Mrs Norris.

I believe the Bible absolutely endorses the importance of giving praise where it is due and of encouraging effort in the right direction. Colossians 3:21 warns fathers not to embitter their children, lest they become discouraged. However, in falling over ourselves to encourage, we might find ourselves using words of praise indiscriminately and overworking the superlatives (which also ultimately devalues the praise, of course). Alongside this habitual commendation there is sometimes an unconscious, fixed reluctance to cause our children pain by a deserved, corrective rebuke. Yet that kind of painful experience is a means of learning. 'Before I was afflicted I went astray, but now I obey your word,' says Psalm 119:67.

So there must be pain to reinforce boundaries. My own childhood memories include an episode which culminated in a very severe telling-off (and more). I can tell you that I did not transgress in the same way again. And if your children cry when they are rebuked, pray that it may be godly sorrow which leads to repentance (2 Corinthians 7:10).

Acknowledgment of sin

But the issues go wider and deeper than the incidence of bad behaviour. Something which should characterise every Christian home is the freely acknowledged fact that every family member is a sinner. As Romans 3:10 proclaims, 'There is none righteous, no, not one' (NKJV). That is one of the many reasons I personally hate behaviour charts with stickers and stars. I believe they encourage self-righteousness and a focus on externals, whereas the fact is that there is a problem deep down in the human heart and that is true of all of us. We need to teach and model to our children sorrow for sin. It is also a problem which only Jesus Christ can sort out. Praise the Lord he has – but at what a cost! Downplaying sin, or calling it something else, will in the end downplay that grace.

As parents we can be very ready to excuse or deny our children's sin. Sometimes sinful behaviour is medicalised and diagnosed as symptomatic of a syndrome, as though that relieves the 'patient' of any responsibility for his or her choices. Of course there is such a thing as illness, which we are right to be sad about and which should be treated by doctors. Sometimes there are physical or physiological contributory factors to antisocial behaviour too. But the big contributory factor to all naughtiness is the human heart, which wants to be god and doesn't want to submit to the ways of the one true and living God. That is something to sober us and make us all sad. 'Grieve, mourn and wail,' as James 4:9 says. It is that serious.

While Mrs Norris of Mansfield Park flattered her nieces where she should have corrected them, causing their moral compass to be faulty, hear the wisdom of Proverbs 28:23–24:

Whoever rebukes a person will in the end gain favour
  rather than one who has a flattering tongue.
Whoever robs their father or mother
  and says, 'It's not wrong,'
  is partner to one who destroys.

Sir Thomas Bertram learned that the hard way, as do many disappointed and troubled parents. Perhaps there is irony in the fact that avoiding teaching our children to sorrow for sin means that our homes will be houses of far worse sorrow later on:

To have a fool for a child brings grief;
  there is no joy for the parent of a godless fool.

(Proverbs 17:21)

Time to confess

Out of the depths I cry to you, Lord;
  Lord, hear my voice.
Let your ears be attentive
  to my cry for mercy.
If you, Lord, kept a record of sins,
  Lord, who could stand?

But with you there is forgiveness;
so that we can, with reverence, serve you.

(Psalm 130: 1–2)

For our families to live the story means that our awareness of more sin than we can handle is not a theoretical idea. Rather, it is evidenced in a daily practice of acknowledging and confessing our failures and weaknesses to each other and to God. One of the bedtime songs my husband and I sang with our children was Bishop Thomas Ken's 'Glory to thee, my God, this night.' It includes the instructive reminder:

Forgive me Lord, for thy dear Son,
The wrong that I this day have done,
That with the world, myself and thee
I, ere I sleep, at peace may be.

It is not healthy for a child to grow up with a disposition to think a little too well of himself. Love your beautiful child to pieces, but don't be blind to the fact that they are a sinner. You need to know that and so do they. Know also that children do not have the monopoly on sin, but are generally less adept than adults at covering it. It therefore is on display – put in the front window, if you like – in all its ugliness and rebellion. Sometimes as I sang Bishop Ken's bedtime prayer for forgiveness with one of our children, it was me that was asking for pardon. We should be unafraid to acknowledge this sad truth to our children. We need a Saviour no less than they. The Lord's Prayer contains the request for forgiveness alongside the one for provision of daily bread. Jesus knew that we never outgrow those needs.

Sorrow for the world

There is another wider facet of the house of sorrow: rightly acknowledged sorrow for the world, which God created good and is ruined by the Fall. That is evidenced every day, not merely in our own hearts and our own homes, but in the world which we observe and in which we participate.

So another daily practice for a family, perhaps over the meal table, could be to review current news, both local and national. While not forgetting to celebrate and enjoy what is good, extraordinary or funny, it is right to pause, acknowledge with sadness and even pray over what is ugly, painful or offensive to God.

Part of wisdom is the recognition of what cannot be cured, except by God's intervention. Life is full of bewildering providences and terrible, hard facts. Sometimes, from our limited perspective, life doesn't make sense. As Ecclesiastes 1:15 and 18 put it:

> *What is crooked cannot be straightened;*
> *   what is lacking cannot be counted …*
> *For with much wisdom comes much sorrow,*
> *   the more knowledge, the more grief.*

Jesus wept at the tomb of Lazarus at the pain and ravages brought by the Fall. We should do no less.

Sowing in tears

I think raising children is brilliant and I frequently encourage parents to enjoy it. But I hope I never hide the fact that parenting also brings pain. It has its tearful side. Many parents will sympathise with those who, having finally got their wayward youngsters into their respective beds, review the day with a heavy heart. It is sobering to be faced with your own failures; it can be shocking to see just how wayward in heart your child is.

Psalm 126:4 is a humble prayer for help, recognising that only God can restore fortunes:

> *Restore our fortunes, LORD,*
> *like streams in the Negev.*

But turn things round he can, for the perspective of this psalm is that God is in the restoration business. He has done it before and it is truly, heart-stoppingly wonderful. The writer can therefore continue with this confidence:

> *Those who sow with tears*
> *will reap with songs of joy.*
>
> (Psalm 126:5)

So a terrible parenting day is not the end of the story. Keep going, patiently asking and trusting God. You have reason to hope. My argument to myself on such days was, 'He saved you, Ann, and you were a selfish, shallow, rude, ungrateful, rebellious, nasty piece of work. So why can't he save your wayward offspring?' Gracious God that he is, he heard those prayers.

> *Those who are wayward in spirit will*
>> *gain understanding;*
>> *those who complain will accept instruction.*
>
> (Isaiah 29:24)

> *People of Zion, who live in Jerusalem, you will weep no more. How gracious he will be when you cry for help!'*
>
> (Isaiah 30:19)

6

A House of Singing

One of the things readers love about the A.A. Milne Pooh stories is the fact that Winnie the Pooh is always making up songs. As he trots along he hums and sings cheerful ditties which form a soundtrack to his adventures.

If a film was being made of your life, what song or piece of music would you choose as its theme tune? You may never have asked yourself that question, but the fact is that lives have a soundtrack. Noel Coward, in his play *Private Lives*, rightly drew attention to the potency of cheap music. The popular comedy series *Peter Kay's Car Share* demonstrates the same thing: the power of the popular song. Kay knows his pop music and, through entertaining fantasy sequences, demonstrates how people take on board those songs and put themselves into them. They take the songs as their own script for life.

Singing should be a huge component and joyfully significant aspect of life in a happy house. Do not underestimate its potency. Songs stay with people and supply glasses through which they see themselves and the world.

It is very biblical to sing. Christianity is the singing faith. There are dozens of injunctions to sing in the Bible, especially in the psalms. Making a joyful noise is something that can and should include people of all ages:

> … *young men and women,*
>   *old men and children.*
> *Let them praise the name of the* LORD.

(Psalm 148:12–13)

Nor is singing something you should only do at church. Living God's story will mean that your whole day is peppered with songs. When Paul encourages the Colossian Christians to get stuck into the Bible so that it permeated their lives, it seems that singing was to be very much part of the process:

Let the message of Christ dwell among you richly as you teach and admonish one another with all wisdom through psalms, hymns, and songs from the Spirit, singing to God with gratitude in your hearts

(Colossians 3:16)

You may protest that you have no musical talent, or that your trombone is gathering dust in the attic. That is of no matter whatsoever. This is not about playing concertos, or being the Von Trapp Family Singers. Think more in terms of Wesley's injunction to congregations that they should 'sing lustily and with good courage'. So stick some songs into your family routines.

When to sing

There are many opportunities for a family to sing throughout the day. Here are a few suggestions:

- Sing at the table to start or close a meal. Perhaps have a song of the week.

- Sing at bedtimes. Lullabies or songs of confession, thankfulness and praise would all be appropriate.

- Sing while you do chores. This was a huge element of folk tradition.

- Sing in the car, especially on long journeys.

What to sing

This, of course, is to some extent a matter of taste. I won't bore the reader with a description of the eclectic Benton family repertoire. Build up your own family collection which makes singing personal and real. Here though are some categories to consider:

- Classic songs which testify to God's work in our lives and tell of his excellent greatness and love. From 'Amazing Grace' to 'In Christ Alone' there is a massive and rich back catalogue of Christian hymnody in a range of musical styles. As such they nourish the soul as they are sung, memorised and internalised. Pass them on.

- Songs which talk of creation, providence and common grace, whether technically 'Christian' or not. I'm thinking of Louis Armstrong's 'What a Wonderful World' as an example. You can dismiss this as sentimental tosh or admit that it touches something deep and special which believers should be the first to celebrate.

- Love songs. There is a sense in which all good love songs are God songs because they echo the gospel in as far as they express tenderness, faithfulness and redemption. Since marriage is a picture of Christ and the church, songs of expectation, commitment and happiness in the relationship between a man and a woman often contain gospel imagery. Examples are Paul Simon's 'Bridge over Troubled Water' and Coldplay's 'Fix You'.

- Songs which celebrate home. These emanate from a longing for heaven, implanted deep in every human heart. An example is John Denver's 'Country Roads'.

- Silly or funny songs with words and sounds to enjoy. Some songs are pure nonsense and can be sung for the joy of it, as a way of expressing shared pleasure at a particular occasion. On the other hand, Colin Buchanan, who has done an immeasurable service for the church through his songs, manages to combine solid truth with a lot of hilarious musical and verbal idioms.

I know that most of the examples reveal my twentieth-century pedigree and perhaps my misspent youth. That is why I shall make no more specific suggestions but urge you to make your own family songbook. The funny and endearing thing is that our children, who were born long after the Beatles had ceased to be, can sing and harmonise many of their songs verbatim. Our daughter even walked down the aisle to 'Here, There and Everywhere'. The parents' songbook is powerful.

It may shock some readers that I cite songs written by unbelievers. Yet in God's common grace there are things within our godless culture that are true, lovely and admirable. And truth is truth wherever it is found. All truth is God's truth. I find it sad when Christians are afraid to be normal. Trust in Christ should make us more beautifully human, not less so.

A particularly delightful aspect of the parents' songbook is to hear some of those same pieces passed on to the next generation. The songs we sang to our children at bedtime are now being sung by those same children in turn to *their* children. Of course they personalise the repertoire by adding in ones which are meaningful to them or their wives/ husbands. Creating their own songbook is part of the folk process.

The power of song

As I have already said, we should sing because it is biblical to do so. Jesus sang (Mark 14:26). We are instructed, 'Sing to the Lord a new song' (Psalm 98:1). Heaven is described as where 'thousands upon thousands' of angels are singing 'in a loud voice' (Revelation 5:11–12). It is a truly heavenly activity, and therefore a way of bringing a little bit of heaven into your home. Singing is also powerful for the following reasons:

- Singing is different from speaking. Something about the combined effort in harnessing breath and vocal muscles triggers emotions. Singing also, so I am told, releases endorphins in the brain. It makes us feel good. In particular, singing together with others has a powerful effect, uniting people simultaneously in common voice to a common end. The conductor and broadcaster Gareth Malone, who has done a great job in promoting the value of choral singing for healing fractured and hurting communities, has proved this point. He has worked wonders with local communities, schools and, famously, military wives. The therapeutic value of such singing is well documented and undeniable. But Christians have been singing for centuries, so let us continue to do so, including at home. Have we not more to sing about and unite us than Liverpool football supporters on the Kop?

- Singing is a fantastic vehicle for conveying truth. As it by definition carries emotion, it is able to combine truth with love. Of course I could tell my children that I love Jesus. But when I often sung at bedtime

'How Sweet the Name of Jesus Sounds', I was telling not just facts about Jesus but something of the depth of what he means to me. As that hymn expresses it:

> *He makes the wounded spirit whole*
> *and charms the troubled breast;*
> *'tis manna to the hungry soul,*
> *and to the weary, rest.*[16]

- Singing is an unsurpassed aid to memory. That is why our children learned the catechism, the books of the Bible and the kings of Judah in song, as well as myriads of Bible verses. These things will stay with them until their deathbed. Having had the honour of attending a number of Christians just before they died, I know how valuable that can be.

To further illustrate the power of song, here is an interesting instance. Anna Warner penned the poem 'Jesus Loves Me, This I Know, for the Bible Tells Me So' in the mid-nineteenth century. Set to a tune by William Bradbury, it was carried round the world by the burgeoning missionary movement of that time. In 1944 John F. Kennedy's patrol torpedo boat collided with a Japanese destroyer. Kennedy and his crew managed to swim to a nearby island, where they were later discovered by natives and rescued. One of the rescued Americans put his arms around the two natives and sang that song. With great emotion, the natives joined in. 'Yes, Jesus loves me: the Bible tells me so.' It remains one of the most profound sentences in the English language.

So we sing as we 'climb' onwards in our Christian journey. I sometimes think there is much we could learn from Winnie the Pooh.

7

A House of Sympathy

But of this, there is no doubt: that the Kettle and the Cricket, at one and the same moment, and by some power of amalgamation best known to themselves, sent, each, his fireside song of comfort streaming into a ray of the candle that shone out through the window, and a long way down the lane. And this light, bursting on a certain person who, on the instant, approached towards it through the gloom, expressed the whole thing to him, literally in a twinkling, and cried, 'Welcome home, old fellow, welcome home …'

(From *The Cricket on the Hearth*
by Charles Dickens)[17]

Charles Dickens wrote frequently and winsomely about the soothing power of a loving home. In his comparatively little-known Christmas short story *The Cricket on the Hearth*, with the personification of the cricket and indeed the kettle, he conveys this power of a loving atmosphere. The home of Mrs Peerybingle, which contained some sorrows, challenges and even guilty secrets, none the less was overwhelmingly one which shouted a welcome even before an incomer opened its door.

A happy house is like that. It is a house of sympathy. The fact is that the world often chews us up and spits us out. But a happy house should attempt to emulate the Father's house in heaven, where tears are dried and sorrows are soothed. It remembers that Jesus was the friend of sinners; he ate with them.

Better a dish of vegetables with love
than a fattened calf with hatred.

(Proverbs 15:17)

A cheerful heart is good medicine,
but a crushed spirit dries up the bones.

(Proverbs 17:22)

How can this be lived out as we live God's story? Here are three suggestions.

Finding perfect windows

When members of the family walk through the door, what do they find? What do they see, hear, smell, taste or touch? This is an opportunity for some really helpful and telling rituals connected to our five senses. Whether that is a kiss and a hug, some soothing music, a cup of hot chocolate, the smell of baking bread or a hearty casserole in the oven, or all of the above, there are many ways in which to say, 'You are welcome and loved here.' I recall one young wife telling me that she had realised that her husband, when he came in from work, liked to see her busy by the cooker. Such an idea might be derided as unreconstructed or chauvinistic, but this godly woman understood it as a way to say, 'Welcome home.' To her immense credit she complied willingly and with a smile. That was the way she lived her story.

Other events invade our homes unexpectedly and even unhappily, perhaps through accidents and illnesses. Yet they can bring joy as new habits are learned or rituals enacted. They are windows of opportunity. A cut knee is a great opportunity for attention and tender care. The cuddle (Mummy's medicine) is a critical part of the healing process. Likewise, illnesses, which can inconvenience other routines and the smooth running of a household, are a wonderful opportunity to demonstrate patterns of care for one another. So let everyone participate in the care of the sufferer, as a matter of principle, training and example. This demonstrates the fact that as a family we look out for each other. A brother, says Proverbs 17:17, 'is born for a time of adversity'.

This is a broken world. People become ill, they suffer, they die. So we model sympathy by weeping with those who weep and comforting those in pain. Little rituals of bringing flowers, food and notes of comfort are all small – but no less meaningful – ways of learning how to show sympathy and love. As appropriate, so is the use of touch. One day my bicycle was stolen, but I was unspeakably comforted by one of my boys, aged only two. Seeing my sadness, he put his little round arms round my neck saying, 'Don't cry, Mummy.' It was worth the loss of the bike.

Creating community through speech

> *The mouth of the righteous is a fountain of life,*
> > *but the mouth of the wicked conceals violence.*
> *Hatred stirs up conflict,*
> > *but love covers over all wrongs.*
> *Wisdom is found on the lips of the discerning,*
> > *but a rod is for the back of one who has no sense.*
> *The wise store up knowledge,*
> > *but the mouth of a fool invites ruin.*

(Proverbs 10:11–14)

This cluster of proverbs demonstrates ways in which God's story is lived through our words. I recall a very bohemian, eco-friendly health food shop run by hippies where the notice by the door read 'Only kindness spoken here.' While one might take issue with the word 'only' in that sentence, it is a very good principle for those who are seeking to live the story. The word of God to us is clothed in grace, and so words spoken in a happy house should have the same tone. Attitudes and words of hatred or of love will either lead to the breaking or building of a community respectively.

However, these proverbs are not saying that we should not correct our children, hence the reference to 'a rod'. There is a place for chastisement; indeed words of hate should not go unchallenged or uncorrected. But the picture painted here is where a person is not looking to be critical, to get others into trouble or to take offence. Speech in a happy house covers wrongs in the sense of seeking peace, not needless strife or disharmony. And grace will enable the parent not to take misbehaviour personally. Part of the ongoing learning curve in a happy house is about how to live in a house full of sinners. What should be written over every front door is: 'We are all sinners here.'

Words, as we know all too well from our own experience, are powerful forces either for building up or tearing down. Habitually thinking of kind words to cheer a person up should be a regular challenge to each family member.

Sorting the siblings

Over the years I have run parenting courses, and second only to questions concerning discipline and behaviour management are questions about sibling rivalry. More or less every parent with more than one child understands the scenario of brotherly bickering and sisterly sniping. It is typical to remark that such behaviour is normal, in the sense of not unusual. But right? Of course not! And of all the things that can truly ruin the peace of a happy house, this is surely number one.

One can take proactive measures to do with timetabling, geographical territory within the house, and giving each individual time and attention. But while such initiatives might calm things down and mitigate the tension, they deal with the surface not the root.

The fact is that God hates sibling rows. Here is one of the sections of Scripture we taught our children to memorise by heart (with actions):

There are six things the Lord hates,
seven that are detestable to him:
haughty eyes,
a lying tongue,
hands that shed innocent blood,
a heart that devises wicked schemes,
feet that are quick to rush into evil,
a false witness who pours out lies

and a person who stirs up conflict in the community.

(Proverbs 6:16–19)

As I explained before, the key to numerical sayings is normally the last item. Therefore it would seem that the follies described in the first six characteristics contribute to the seventh. In other words, bad feeling between siblings is stirred up by other things that have been going on.

Our children need to be raised in the mantra that peace in the family is precious because that is what God desires. Knowing the different elements that disrupt communal peace might help parents to put in place, and train children in, habits to counter such destructive practices.

These start with thinking too highly of oneself and proceed to lies and exaggeration. Unfair dealings which cause needless grief therefore need to be replaced by fair and loving practices. This does take practice. As the heart that devises wicked schemes is the one concerned only with self, training in thinking of others, even with the common courtesies of table manners, is useful. Such practices declare that a happy house thinks of others first. Small, everyday rituals are the training for a house of sympathy. Certain acts and attitudes, like slander and gossip for example, will then become naturally taboo.

Like the cricket in Dickens' story, such good habits, when particularly reinforced and encouraged, will send out a stream of warm and welcoming light. They will make not only every family member feel glad to be home and instantly relieved, but will also impact the stranger who is welcomed as an angel unawares.

8

A House of Service

You know that the household of Stephanas were
the first converts in Achaia, and they have devoted
themselves to the service of the Lord's people.

(1 Corinthians 16:15)

Here in this Scripture is a family who are living the
story. The household of Stephanas may or may
not have included children, but the people who
made up that household are famous collectively
for their devoted service to other Christians. It was
a thing they did together. Note that the precursor
to all this is that they were converted people and
therefore were followers of Jesus, who 'did not
come to be served, but to serve, and to give his
life as a ransom for many' (Mark 10:45). So they
learned to serve from the Master.

The children of our households may not yet be converted, but a happy house can train them in the art and the joy of service. This should be a huge part of the subculture of the Christian home. The world tends to be more concerned instead with children's self-image. Go to your local bookshop and you will find plenty of books on building your child's self-esteem, but you are unlikely to find one on teaching your child to serve.

From their earliest years children should see a husband who delights to serve his wife, expressing true manhood in the way he protects her and attends to her needs. Equally they should witness a wife who takes pleasure in serving her husband, demonstrating respect in the things she does for him. Children will then readily imitate and participate in little deeds of kindness for another. This could be through kitchen chores, household errands, sorting out the computer, thoughtfulness at the table or caring for some family member who is wounded and weary. Small acts of unselfishness should always be commended.

Church as a place of service

But serving your family is a bit like serving yourself. The household of Stephanas no doubt excelled at serving each other and made each other very happy when they did. However, that is not what they are commended for by the apostle Paul. They 'devoted themselves to the service of the Lord's people', that is the local church, which would have included all kinds of people, of all ages and backgrounds. No doubt some were those whom the world would call 'odd'. Churches have plenty of those, and rightly so because I think Jesus would have made a point of extending love to them. He gave a serious challenge to his disciples about not limiting your love to those who are easy to love and will readily love you back: 'And if you greet only your own people, what are you doing more than others? Do not even pagans do that?' (Matthew 5:47).

So how great a priority for you and your family is church? Is it just included in the routines with all the significance of a swimming lesson or a visit to the dentist? Is it something you use as a lifestyle enhancement? Or do you consider your biological family as a little circle within the bigger circle of church family?

The family in Psalm 128 had a Zion focus. All their hopes were in God's kingdom. The New Testament too considers church more important than family. Note how Paul, in all of his letters, when he comes to application, deals with application to the church first. Ephesians is an example of this. The ultimate family is God's family.

Although old country and western or gospel songs were full of allusions to the reuniting of an earthly family in heaven – with words such as 'Tell Mother I'll be there!' – those earthly bonds will dissolve at death. But the church of God, the city of God – which will gloriously include people of all races and backgrounds, as well as those who had large families and those who had none – is what will remain. We see in Ephesians 5 that the church is Christ's bride. He died to save her. Church, of which your local church is a part, is important.

Choosing a church

The poet John Betjeman wrote a quirky little story called *Archie and the Strict Baptists*. I came upon it the year my husband was called into the ministry of a Strict Baptist (now Grace Baptist) church, and was intrigued. Archie, the protagonist of the story, is a teddy bear who loves chapel. He is made seriously unhappy when his owners move house and he can't get to the chapel, with its Aneucapnic lamps, he had known and loved. For a long time he and his friend Jumbo (an elephant, of course) are stuck away in a cupboard.

One evening somebody came to look in the cupboard where Archie and Jumbo lived, carrying an Aneucapnic lamp. The memories the lamp stirred up in the poor old animal were more than he could bear. He determined to go to chapel – somehow.[18]

The story goes on to describe how the determined Archie makes himself a pair of brown paper wings so that every Sunday morning he can fly to a local chapel where they have really good, long sermons.

It's all very fanciful and ridiculous, but I have to say I like Archie's style. Church is important, and so is choosing the church of which you will be a part. In fact, this is far more important for parents than choosing a school. Apart from all your children will learn there (hopefully all solid truth), you are choosing a community in which they can learn to serve. So look for a place where there are opportunities to be connected into the family of God. Look for a place to give not merely to gain.

James K.A. Smith comments on this subject:

Looking for the coolest or most popular youth group might not be the best indicator of where our children will be conformed to the image of Christ. To the contrary, it might be the 'boring' congregation that actually does more to shape their loves and longing precisely by rehearsing the biblical story, week in and week out, in practices that are at work on their hearts even if they don't realise it.[19]

Smith particularly has in mind, but not exclusively, spoken liturgy as well as the routines and practices of a church community outside the service itself. In our family experience these were especially significant in shaping the loves and longings of our children's developing mind and heart.

Likewise, sometimes a smaller church will tick more of the boxes. The household of Stephanas, being the first converts in Achaia, must have begun church life in a small church.

The routines of church life

What are the church routines you can embrace into your family as something that you (plural) do in learning and loving to serve? Here are some ideas which might become much-loved family traditions:

- Children being really committed in their attendance of church youth activities.

- Older children playing with little ones.

- Pushing a wheelchair for a disabled member, opening doors, or fetching and carrying items.

- Serving coffee after services.

- Cleaning the church building – whether on a rota or on an annual spring-cleaning day.

- Decorating the church for Christmas.

- Helping with a children's Holiday
  Bible Club

- Helping at an event for seniors, such as a
  Holiday at Home.

Leviticus 19 lists injunctions concerning good habits for God's people. For example, 'Do not curse the deaf or put a stumbling-block in front of the blind' (verse 14) and 'Stand up in the presence of the aged, show respect for the elderly' (verse 32). These were actions to inculcate an attitude of service, honour and compassion.

What a gift to a child to have these opportunities to love and serve across generations. How endearing to witness them. And how the children enjoy them, stuffing them into their bank of memories and being shaped by them. Just as Stephanas and his two mates (perhaps his sons?) refreshed Paul when they visited him (1 Corinthians 16:17), I have witnessed elderly saints being refreshed by the sweet, unaffected conversation of a child at church.

Serving the community

We also all live in neighbourhoods. Though these are probably less of a community than they ought to be or once were, as a family we can enjoy doing our bit. Are there random, or even specific, acts of kindness in which your family can get involved and by which you can serve your community? My heart was warmed one day when I walked through a subway not far from our home and witnessed a local Christian family cleaning nasty graffiti off the walls. Another way of serving would be to go out 'wombling' locally and see who can collect most litter from the local park or streets.

In the newspaper last year I read of a mother who, every Christmas, makes a different sort of advent calendar for her children. Underneath every number is detailed an act of kindness to perform that day: make a Christmas card for the binmen; take tins to the food bank with Mummy; find three toys to donate to the charity shop; sing carols for a neighbour; and so on. As the writer of the article comments:

None of the acts are going to change the world. In fact they are largely symbolic – little prompts to encourage them to slow down and remember that the world does not revolve around our Christmas wish lists.[20]

So live the storyline of service. This will help to counter the heightened sense of entitlement which is endemic in our current prevailing culture. It is not our children's fault – many have been systematically taught to put no one above themselves. Everything is measured as to how it makes them feel. Nearly every photograph is a selfie. Something has to be in it for them. But that is precluded if you understand the gospel. And that understanding can be enhanced for the growing child if, as a family, you have built in ways of demonstrating what it is to serve.

A house of service is also the road to a healthy, happy and liberating self-forgetfulness. It might even be the road for your children coming to Christ – the great Servant of all.

9

A House of Sharing

The popular film *Paddington* could be seen as a moral fable on the subject of generosity and hospitality. The bear arrives in England from Darkest Peru with high expectations of British courtesy and hoping to find a friend, only to be profoundly disappointed as he sits, ignored, on Paddington station. He feels abandoned and alone. When the Brown family alight from the train, Mr Brown's instinct, and instruction, is to give the bear a very wide berth indeed. 'Stranger Danger!' is code for 'Don't get involved.' It is Mrs Brown's soft heart and generous impulse that swings things in Paddington's favour. And so Paddington finds a home.

Mr Brown is driven by fear. He has a heightened risk awareness (very familiar to anyone in the twenty-first century who has been bewildered by current health and safety regulations, which appear at times to have said 'goodbye' to common sense). Fear often prevents sharing because sharing contains an inbuilt risk of someone taking advantage of you. It is safer to keep all your possessions to yourself. It is safer to lock your door against strangers. That way your carpets will not get muddied; your fridge will not get emptied; no one will make a fool of you.

However, it was hardly 'safe' for the Son of God to come to earth and to face the extremes of human brutality on a cross of execution:

For you know the grace of our Lord Jesus Christ, that though he was rich, yet for your sake he became poor, so that you through his poverty might become rich.

(2 Corinthians 8:9)

Paul uses the example of Jesus to encourage generous, cheerful giving. Living God's story means giving because of what Christ gave for us. So a happy house must be a house of sharing.

King David understood this idea of grace. When he finally became King of Israel, he put out a clear message of grace. The first act of most new sovereigns was to exterminate all their enemies and rivals to the crown. This purge would extend to all known relations. But David sought out the lame grandson of his former enemy, Saul, and provided a home and sustenance for him from his own table. It was the keeping of a promise he had made to Jonathan; it was also a message of grace. Such a stand is appropriate to all recipients of grace.

This chapter is a somewhat nuanced extension of the last. If chapter eight was particularly about our attitude to people, this one is about attitudes to possessions and what is really important. So what might be the routines or rhythms of a house of sharing?

Ownership is OK

Of course you have to feel that you actually own stuff before you can learn to give it away. The Bible commends and defends ownership – hence, for example, the eighth commandment about not stealing and the tenth commandment about not coveting. The Bible does not support the communist idea that property is theft.

God allows us to enjoy the fruit of our labour and he provides us with much in this life to enjoy. We live in a material world. The resurrection of Christ tells us that heaven itself will be material. So it is not sinful to heartily enjoy what God provides (1 Timothy 6:17). On the contrary, it would be churlish to dismiss God's gifts with a shrug, perhaps commenting, 'I care nothing for such baubles.' How rude! Enjoy life from God's hand. Eat and drink and be glad, receiving such gifts with thankfulness. But avoid a grasping attitude. Beware of the lie that tells you that you somehow deserve these things, or are better than other people who don't have them. And beware of becoming self-sufficient so that you think that you don't need God any more.

'Give me neither poverty nor riches,' said a wise man (Proverbs 30:8). One way to avoid the traps of materialism is to celebrate the abundance you have from God's hand. Live without worry or fear, says Jesus in the Sermon on the Mount, because you can trust your heavenly Father to provide what you need (Matthew 6:25–34). And, being grateful and content with what you have, look for ways to share with others, whether that is your possessions, your time, your space or your money.

A door with hinges and a lock

I have taken the above phrase from Edith Schaeffer. The Schaeffer family really did know how to open their home to friends and strangers alike by swinging wide their front door on its hinges. In turn they realised immense blessing. By investing time, space and their very selves in others, they saw lives turned around to the glory of God. Their home was enriched as the whole family got to know people from a vast range of cultures and backgrounds.

If you have space in your car on an outing, whom could you take along? Do you have too much food? Invite some people to share it. These things are a modern equivalent of the Old Testament rule about not gleaning to the very edge of your field (Leviticus 19:9–10). Leave something for the poor.

Such habits remind us of the principle behind hospitality – a wonderfully enriching activity in which the whole family can be involved. This is true whether it is in the kitchen, stirring the gravy; or in the sitting room, entertaining the company with offerings from the 1000 best jokes book; or around the table, with its inbuilt message of acceptance and belonging.

Sharing such routines does not mean that your children have to feel that their lives are permanently invaded. The gleaning principle also protected the rights of the owner of the field and those who benefited from being regular workers in it. While the door has hinges to swing wide open, it also has a lock. In the rhythms of family life there are times for inclusion, but also times rightly for exclusion so that no one need feel threatened, resentful or exhausted.

Baking and making

God the Creator has made us creative in a myriad different ways. Harness this creative impulse in making things to serve or cheer others. Remember the example of Dorcas, who was famous for making clothes for people (Acts 9:39). Dressmaking, painting, cooking, decorating, gardening, singing, playing an instrument, writing, model-making – all kinds of gifts can be used in a pleasurable way.

Paddington Bear gets the whole Brown family making marmalade. I know families who also have a marmalade day – a shared cottage industry with an end-product which others are glad to receive. Others bake then set up a stall outside their house to sell their produce to raise funds for charity. A family cooking session could result in fun dropping off food to those who might need or enjoy it. Those who love to garden might grow flowers, fruit or vegetables to give away. Children who love making cards could make ones for those who are sick or sad.

The list is endless. Yet a generous habit takes practice.

Habitual giving away

I heard that one family's routine was for the children to tithe their weekly pocket money and put it in a jar. When the jar was full, the coins were counted. Then the family, in conference, chose the charity or organisation to which they would donate. But here's the fun part: the deal was that however much the children had collected, the father would multiply it by ten as his additional contribution to the chosen recipient. All this generated great happiness in the giving and a shared pleasure in collaborative generosity.

Some families regularly sort out cupboards and give away surplus toys and clothes to a needy family or to a charity shop. Funnily enough, when you give away like this, you generate not just cupboard space but love capacity. Other families enjoy making up parcels for missionaries. Someone who grew up this way said there were always parcels in the hall waiting to be sent abroad. It left an indelible impression.

There are always serious questions to challenge the Christian family. How much is enough? What shall we do with our surplus? Is upwardly mobile the only direction? These are not questions that I can answer for you. But I can commend that you regularly ask them of yourselves and pray over the answers.

A culture of abundance

A child came home from school with a question for her mother. Apparently some of the children at school had been talking about what jobs their respective parents did. There had been general shock when this particular child had revealed that her mother had no paid employment. The consensus was that this child's family must be very rich. Hence the child's question: 'Mummy, are we rich?' In fact, this was a Christian family who had a meagre bank balance but had decided to live on one wage for the sake of other advantages to the family. The mother thought for a moment before she answered the question with a smile: 'Yes, we are rich.'

The family of a happy house should always think of themselves as rich. They have the treasure which is Christ. And they are invited to be rich in good deeds.

This culture of abundance lends naturally to including other people. So young, single or older people become adopted into the family as surrogate sisters, aunts, grandmas and granddads. Everybody wins.

When our youngest child was a newborn baby, I heard that a blind woman who lived nearby had lost her husband and was desperately lonely. I dared to knock on her door and introduce myself in this rather gauche way: 'Hello, my name's Ann and I live down the road. I've just had a baby. Would you like to hold him?' She did like, and so began a routine of regular visits. She held and rocked the baby while I made the tea and we chatted. Then when the baby was too big to be held, he crawled on the floor while we chatted more. And so the years went by and she started coming to our home, church and other events. It became our habit for me to read the Bible to her and pray with her. Inclusion led to witness.

'Charity begins at home', so the old saying goes. People who state that are usually looking to justify stinginess. But charity, that is gospel charity, really does begin at home in a house of sharing with outsiders. This in itself increases the sense of having an abundance. The blessing extends outwards and boomerangs back.

A generous person will prosper;
*   whoever refreshes others will be refreshed.*

(Proverbs 11:25)

That is what the Brown family discovered. Even the wallpaper in the Brown hallway blossomed.

10

A House of Sojourn

The song 'You'll Never Walk Alone' did not start life as a football anthem. It was written by Oscar Hammerstein and set to music by Richard Rodgers as a literal showstopper, the big finish to the musical *Carousel*.

Carousel has a rather peculiar plotline. It follows the careers of two factory girls, Carrie and Julie. Carrie marries the entrepreneurial fisherman Enoch Snow and goes on to have a tribe of children. The whimsical Julie makes an impulsive marriage to a vagabond fairground man called Billy. He treats Julie badly, gets involved in shady dealings and is killed when a robbery goes wrong. He leaves Julie pregnant and never meets his daughter. Arriving in heaven (as you do?), Billy is filled with self-loathing and regret. After arguing his case with someone polishing a star, he is allowed back to earth to see how his family are getting on. Years have passed: his daughter is now a teenager, dealing with bullying and social ostracism. At her graduation the school principal gives a homily, which is this famous song, 'when you walk through the storm hold your head up high and don't be afraid of the dark … walk on through the wind, walk on through the rain'. Its message is 'hold your head up' and keep going through the tough times because, as it concludes, 'you'll never walk alone'. There's not a dry eye in the house as the curtain comes down.

So far, all the elements of a happy house may have sounded as though things will go on the same way forever. Indeed, a house sounds like a static, fixed thing. But even in Psalm 128 there is the notion of movement as the head of the house is described as walking in the Lord's ways, moving on with God.

Actually, a happy house is more like an inn on the road, a place of sojourn, a temporary residence for pilgrims – those who fear the Lord.

Blessed are those whose strength is in you,
  whose hearts are set on pilgrimage.

(Psalm 84:5)

The pilgrim days will pass swiftly and then comes the real house where God's people will live eternally – the forever home.

... and I will dwell in the house of the LORD
  for ever.

(Psalm 23:6)

This is what truly marks out those who are living the story. They know that on earth they have no continuing city. They are living with eternity in view.

While *Carousel* is a great musical with very dodgy theology, its closing song has the power to move the human spirit because it chimes in with a deep human longing, placed there by the God who made us. 'He has ... set eternity in the human heart' (Ecclesiastes 3:11). That statement comes after the famous poem about time – 'a time for everything' – with its clock-like rhythm, reminding us of time's unstoppable march.

There is no return. Every activity has a use-by date. And yet we have, hardwired into us, a sense of eternity.

A Christian family walking in God's ways will keep this concept very much in mind. They will know that they are a house of sojourn, on a journey, trapped on a carousel of time, as the seasons go round and one year succeeds another. But (and this is the big deal which prevents this chapter from getting maudlin) because of Jesus, who entered time from eternity and went through death and out the other side, the journey of life is transformed to one not from cradle to grave, but from grace to glory.

So residents of a house of sojourn wear their travelling shoes. Here are some of the attitudes and habits of the best kind of travellers.

A robust sense of adventure

Recall the song John Bunyan wrote about Christian on his journey from the City of Destruction to the Celestial City:

> *Who would true valour see?*
> *Let him come hither;*

One here will constant be
Come wind, come weather.
There's no discouragement
Shall make him once relent
His first avowed intent
To be a pilgrim.

The song reeks of daring, determination and joy. Sometimes our children are presented with an invitation to follow Christ which sounds about as interesting and inactive as a game of 'dead lions' (a party game devised by weary adults who want a quiet life with sleepy children). John Bunyan knew different with his 'who dares wins' attitude to the Christian life, and we should recapture that as we talk to our children about our own walk with God.

Do we inspire our children to embrace the adventure of following Jesus, or is it presented as a dull but necessary and slightly namby-pamby expedient? Away with such a dastardly lie! It is grand to be a Christian. This is literally the journey of a lifetime.

A refusal to be too much encumbered

While recently visiting members of our family in Japan, we had occasion to travel on crowded Tokyo trains. You don't know crowded trains until you have journeyed on the Tokyo underground at rush hour. If you want to make it extra difficult, try having a massive suitcase and a number of other bags. That is a journey of sheer endurance that you won't repeat in a hurry.

With eternity in view, we don't need to travel like this: over-encumbered with this world's stuff. I don't just mean material goods either, but all that we can fill our lives chasing.

Try walking round a graveyard with your children. Read some of the names there and guess at some of the stories. Perhaps, more instructively, note those gravestones where time and weather have obliterated the names. Life is short and uncertain, and most of us will not even remain in people's memories long.

If such a practice is morbid, it is so only to those whose total focus is on their worldly ambitions: A levels, degrees, sporting success, a big bank balance, a flourishing career, a wonderful house and extraordinary children. Who will care about those things ultimately, even though they are read out as accolades at your funeral? You won't be there to bask in the glory. On the other hand, to see those things in their right perspective, the Bible's perspective, is totally liberating. It might, for example, liberate a mother from the chains which bind her to an ambitious and lucrative career path because she wants to invest her talents in the less glamorous but more important work of raising her children. It might liberate you, your time and your money from filling every waking moment of your children's lives so that their future CVs will outshine those of other applicants to Oxbridge. It will certainly liberate you to enjoy the experience and delights, great and small, God has given you of simply being alive on this day.

So a house of sojourn enables us to have a healthy and balanced view of what life offers and makes us more willing to share. Discover the joys of travelling light.

A relish of the ride

To be a sojourner does not mean you cannot enjoy the country you are travelling through.

On the contrary, a journey affords so much to observe and savour, as the Bible commands us to do:

> *Light is sweet,*
>   *and it pleases the eyes to see the sun.*
> *However many years anyone may live,*
>   *let them enjoy them all.*

(Ecclesiastes 11:7–8)

So model and teach your children to delight in small, even momentary pleasures. These are God's gift to us as much as the sunrise each day. Or maybe your children can teach you this – and you should be careful not to drive this out of them. Take a small child for a walk round the block and see how slow they can be, not because their legs are short, but because they stop to look at an ant going down the crack in the pavement, or a digger in the road, or a bird in the sky. And they will probably collect a precious stick or two. We do not always have to be driven from one appointment to the next, nor to see each day as a series of hoops we have to negotiate. From the first cup of tea to the turning out of the light as you snuggle into a warm bed, every day affords so many small pleasures. Teach your children to acknowledge them, smile at them and remember who gave them to us. Gratitude is a great habit to cultivate.

We can also enjoy all this while accepting it as transitory. We know it is not the real deal because we live with eternity in view. This changes everything. It will enable us to enjoy our lives, our possessions and our relationships without making too much of them. We keep a pilgrim spirit.

Of course we must be clear about this. We cannot plonk our children's feet onto the narrow way. They have to step on it themselves. In *Pilgrim's Progress* Christian set out from the City of Destruction alone. His wife and children followed later. There is what Dale Ralph Davis calls 'the continuing emergency of our faith'[21] – an urgency that each succeeding generation must embrace truly and heartily for themselves, not merely knowing about the Lord but knowing the Lord. 'Circumcise your hearts,' was the cry of many an Old Testament prophet. We cannot do that for our children.

But we can live in such a way that demonstrates no ultimate satisfaction with what this world and this life has to offer. We can smile and thoroughly enjoy the moment, but always in the knowledge that this is good as far as it goes. The best is yet to come.

A resolution through adversity

The day I was working on this chapter our car broke down somewhere in Gloucestershire. We sat on a grass verge a very long time while the traffic whizzed by, waiting to be rescued. This was a useful reminder to me that all journeys are hazardous and will include a certain amount of inconvenience. It can be all extremely tiresome. But the pilgrim spirit equips you to 'walk on through the rain' in the knowledge that you really do not journey by yourself.

Perhaps Oscar Hammerstein's Jewish background was what was consciously or unconsciously behind the lyric about never walking alone. It certainly echoes Psalm 23:

Even though I walk
through the darkest valley,

I will fear no evil,
for you are with me ...

(Psalm 23:4)

The Bible tells us much more clearly and solidly than Hammerstein that although life's path will include some dark days, we have a companion who will not desert us. Teach your children this and you give them the essential equipment for a life into which some rain will certainly fall. Model too turning to that Saviour-Friend in prayer.

Furthermore, as Ecclesiastes 3 tells us, the seasons of our life come to pass. We will be able to walk on. Hobgoblins and foul fiends are par for the course, as Bunyan's Pilgrim discovered. But his spirit was undaunted: 'We know we, at the end, shall life inherit.' My family had a pictorial representation of the road travelled by Christian in *Pilgrim's Progress* hanging on our dining-room wall. It served as a reminder of the inevitable ups and downs and ins and outs of all our journeys. Only trust in a sovereign, loving God, who orders things for our good – even when we can't see how or why – enables us to sit trouble out, face it down or even embrace it.

A remembrance of the destination

What gets you through an arduous journey? Of course it is the thought that you will ultimately get to your destination and then the holiday really starts. You remember where you are going.

I recently had some of my grandchildren to stay. After they were scrubbed and in their pyjamas ready for bed, they were allowed down to the sofa for 'Granny's Film Club'. Over a number of evenings we watched the now ancient film version of Patricia St John's classic *The Tanglewoods' Secret*.[22] It is the story of a strong-willed little girl who, through a series of unfortunate events, comes to repentance and faith. As such it is an instructive, heart-warming and sensitive portrayal of a child's conversion to Christ. But there is another strand to the story. A boy is seriously injured as the result of a fall from the tree. The little girl tells him about the Saviour and he too trusts Christ. When he subsequently dies (sorry about the spoiler), the girl is perplexed as to how and why God would let that happen. There follows a beautiful conversation with a wise old shepherd who explains the glory that is heaven and why to be there with Jesus is not loss but gain. I commend both the book and the film very highly.

Death happens and even children are sometimes faced with it. Our instinct these days might be to shield them or to talk sentimental waffle. But this is the time for the gospel. Christians never need be afraid to talk about death. Take your children to a Christian funeral, as appropriate, and let them witness resurrection triumph there. Ecclesiastes 7 points out that such an experience is more salutary than a party.

This eternal perspective may also help parents to prioritise how time and money should be spent. So many experiences are available to children these days, many of which have merit. But when there is a choice between A or B, it is always worth considering which course of action or choice of activity is most likely to bear eternal fruit. A posh foreign holiday or a Christian camp? A football club which trains on Sunday or a pattern of regular attendance at church? Take the long view, the eternal perspective.

There will in fact be a party in heaven, a true feast at the marriage supper of the Lamb. An old grace which used to be sung at mealtimes is a wonderful reminder of this:

Be present at our table, Lord;
Be here and everywhere adored.
These mercies bless, and grant that we
May feast in paradise with thee.

Every feast, every gathering together around the table, is a pointer that we are one step nearer that great feast. That is another reason why the family meal table is so special. Light candles, put out flowers, enjoy good food and meet each other's eyes in regular acknowledgment of that wonderful truth.

We will feast in the house of Zion,
We will sing with our hearts restored.
'He has done great things,' we will say together;
We will feast and weep no more.[23]

Our journey is the journey home to the true happy house.

Conclusion: The Fruitful Home

I was going to title this book *The Homemakers*, but I did not want anyone to think it was about making curtains. Also, I did not want to sound too exclusively feminine, for I hope I have demonstrated that homemaking is a job for husband and wife, for mother and father, contributing within their distinct roles. The best of masculine and feminine, according to God's design, will combine to a balanced and beautiful whole. Furthermore, it is a job that can use a little attention from all who are truly passionate about raising godly offspring. Since God is passionate about that (Malachi 2:15), surely any parent who is saved by grace and made alive in Christ will want to aspire to the same.

Nevertheless, we are building and furnishing a house. We are preparing a soil in which children will grow and thrive, becoming healthy, strong and blessed by God.

Of course we know the truth of Psalm 127:1:

Unless the LORD builds the house,
the builders labour in vain.

Nothing will be achieved without daily, urgent, prayerful dependence upon him, the Master Builder, the Head Gardener. But the builders are none the less supposed to labour at their house-building, not keep sloping off to have a cup of tea.

The wise woman builds her house,
but with her own hands the foolish one
tears hers down.

(Proverbs 14:1)

The above proverb includes the observation that homes can also be places of destruction. The expression 'broken home' has gone out of fashion due to political correctness, but

I think we all understand the concept. This book has been about making a home which remains unbroken, functional and nourishing so that in the future blessing accumulates with compound interest.

We know that every family generates its own unconscious, unarticulated subculture, for better or worse. The chapters of this book have been written to encourage Christian believers to review and evaluate what they have generated, even unintentionally. Are the structure and the substance and the story there? Are those things evidenced in routines characterised by, as appropriate, sorrow, singing, sympathy, service, sharing and sojourn?

I hasten to add that there is nothing formulaic about this. What is wonderful about a thriving family life is that it is so very personal, unique in fact, to that particular home. You can develop your own delightful ways of expressing sympathy, welcoming strangers, spending Sunday, and serving the church and your community. Make your own kind of unique magic. But be intentional about the patterns and routines you allow to become embedded. This may take some time, effort and energy, and at certain seasons of the parental lives something may have to give.

There may have to be a trade-off of the good for the better. Sometimes too outsiders may not understand your choices and priorities, but they are not the audience that matters. Remember that 'all that is gold does not glitter'. And not all who wander away from the pursuit of worldly ambitions are lost.

As this book has hopefully made clear, a Christian home worthy of the name is more than saying grace at meals and reading a Bible story at bedtime. Whatever the circumstances, bring on the homemakers.

Pass on the baton of truth

This book has majored on the strands of family life which most mark out an effective counterculture to our secular age. Think of the days of the Judges and how things went from bad to worse. Why? Because the generation after Judges allowed the prevailing idolatrous culture to pervade their homes and their lives. Due to fear and compromise they did not complete the job God gave them.

The result was a widespread forgetting of God and apostasy. A happy house it was not.

As twenty-first-century Christians, we are driven back by a militant intolerance of Bible truth and those who adhere to it. Maybe a time will come where family culture will be the only place where we preserve gospel truth and pass on the baton. And even if times don't get that tough yet for the church, know that our children are suffering the relentless battering of humanistic atheism – a worldview which robs children not just of transcendence but of hope, purpose, joy and grace. So rediscover the vision of Psalm 128. Don't dismiss it as twee and unrealistic, but prayerfully pursue it.

The recent film *Dunkirk* had as its advertising strapline 'Survival is victory'. The Christian faith is not in retreat, but crucial to the survival of the truth is that it is passed on from one generation to the next. When this occurs, it is victorious.

Take seriously God's word

Another essential calling of a homemaker is to take seriously God's word. Hear the challenge of 1 Peter 2:11–12:

*Dear friends, I urge you, as foreigners and exiles,
to abstain from sinful desires, which wage war
against your soul. Live such good lives among
the pagans that, though they accuse you of
doing wrong, they may see your good deeds and
glorify God on the day he visits us.*

Jesus knew his disciples had to live and work in the world. We live our family lives before our non-Christian neighbours, not hiding from the world. Christian family culture can make non-Christians envious. We hope it also makes them curious.

We delight in our children, and rightly so. Yet the Old Testament prophet Micah has some sobering words for doting parents:

*Shave your head in mourning
 for the children in whom you delight ...
 for they will go from you into exile.*

(Micah 1:16)

This was a generation who had not taken God seriously. They had a ho-hum attitude to the prophets and thought their words were for other people, not them. That resulted in a heartbreaking legacy. David Prior writes, 'What we bequeath to our children, in whom we profess to take delight, is the acid test of how seriously we are prepared to take the word of God.'[24]

Keep yourselves from idols

The besetting and most damning sin of Old Testament Israel was idolatry. It lost them the Promised Land.

An important caveat to this book, whose theme has been making a home, is to beware of idolising it. There will, no doubt, be times in your family life when your heart swells with joy as you look around you: surrounded by your children at the table, relishing a hearty meal; or snuggled in bed with a ripping yarn; or singing your heads off as you motor down the A303. You might think, 'I really, really *love* this.' Savour those moments and store them in your memory, but remember they are God's gift to you and worship him.

Idolatry of the family, which will often be shot through with personal pride, bears only bad fruit. Like Shakespeare's King Lear, your family life may be throbbing with soaring poetry, but if it is based on deceit, things will come to a sorry end. Jesus warned against such idolatry (Matthew 10:37–39); it is an insult to God, the bane of local churches and a recipe for disaster.

A house of salvation

If you have understood the gospel at all, you will desire above everything else that your home is a house of salvation. Like Eunice and Lois (2 Timothy 1:5; 3:15), you will ensure that from infancy your children know the Holy Scriptures. Like the people who brought their children to Jesus (Mark 10:13–16), you will eagerly urge him to put his hands on them and bless them.

Then, if you are like me, throughout the child-rearing years you will be watching for signs of spiritual growth. When your child is keen to pray his own prayer, you will be glad; when he rolls around the floor during the Bible story, you will be sad. When she begs to be allowed to go to evening service, you will be delighted; when she begs to be excused, you will be discouraged.

At the annual Holiday Bible Club run by my church, there is a tradition following the talk on the third day (of four). Children are invited, if they wish, to place their name badge in a box as an indication that they would like to learn in more detail what it means to follow Jesus and how to become a Christian. Those children will then be counselled in small groups by dedicated leaders on the last day of the club. I have done this over dozens of years and it is an immense privilege. From it I have learned that there are three main reasons why children put their badges in the box.

They want attention. They know that this action gets the warm approval from leaders that they crave.

They want assurance. They have already trusted in Jesus and want to know that they are still on the right track. Or maybe as their understanding has grown, they find this a good way of demonstrating the response of a continuing and expanding faith. Many children from Christian families would be in that category.

They want a Saviour. These are those in whom, praise God, the Holy Spirit has been working in a new way. They may have read the words of the Bible before, they may have previously heard the gospel, but now they take it to heart, recognising the urgency of their need.

Then there are also those, some of whom believe, who for their own reasons do not see the need to put their badge in the box.

It can be the same in the Christian home over the child-rearing years. Some approval-seeking children will regularly draw pictures with crosses and the words 'Jesus' and 'God', because they have learned that Mummy and Daddy like that kind of thing. Some children from an early age take seriously every gospel invitation, explicit or implicit, and walk a steady path of growing faith without knowing precisely 'the hour I first believed'. Some children have a crisis where they are desperate to get right with God. Others might be private and inscrutable over many years, leaving their parents wondering from the sidelines.

Wise parents will know to treat all these manifestations, or the lack of them, in a measured way. 'Meet with triumph and disaster, and treat those two imposters just the same', as Rudyard Kipling advised.[25] Only God truly knows what is going on in the heart.

Be encouraging about positive indications, but don't go bananas. Likewise, don't think 'game over' or rant, rave and nag if you note negative indications, but let them drive you to ever more prayer. You are on holy ground. Let God do his work. He works in the lives of both children and adults in myriad ways.

A wise older woman once said to me, 'It's not what they are when they are nine or ten, but what they are when they are nineteen and twenty.' Remember the soil metaphor and imitate the patience of a gardener. Don't go poking around the roots, but attend to the soil. Keep it moist and nourishing, and wait for the harvest.

In the introduction to this book I suggested we think about the soil in which our children grow. We should take God seriously in attending to this subject. Then, by the grace of God and in answer to our prayers, our children will put down deep roots into the soil, which the frost of atheism will never reach. Deep roots, as Tolkien so elegantly put it, are not reached by the frost.[26]

The LORD will write in the register of the peoples:
'This one was born in Zion.'

As they make music they will sing,
   'All my fountains are in you.'

(Psalm 87:6–7)

Endnotes

Introduction: What Is a Family?

1. Edith Schaeffer, *What Is a Family?* (Baker Books, 1975).

Part A. Foundations: Building the House

2. Antoine de Saint-Exupéry, *The Wisdom of the Sands* (1945).

2. A House of Structure

3. Robert Frost, 'Mending Wall' (David Nutt, 1914).

4. Anthony Trollope, *Rachel Ray* (Chapman & Hall, 1863).

5. David Gibson, *Destiny* (Inter-Varsity Press, 2016).

3. A House of Substance

6. Kenneth Grahame, *The Wind in the Willows* (Methuen, 1908).

7. Edmund Gosse, *Father and Son* (W. Heinemann, 1907).

8. These are now published under the title *Ferdinand: The Engine That Went Off the Rails* (Christian Focus, 2009).

9. Those two stories are unpublished but other writers have since attempted the same kind of thing.

10. James K.A. Smith, *You Are What You Love* (Brazos Press, 2016).

4. A House of Story

11. Dorothy Canfield Fisher, *The Home-maker* (Persephone Books, 1952).

12. Gosse, *Father and Son*.

13. Gladys Hunt, *Honey for a Child's Heart* (Zondervan, 2002).

14. John Bunyan, *Pilgrim's Progress* (1678).

5. A House of Sorrow

[15.] Jane Austen, *Mansfield Park* (Thomas Egerton, 1814).

6. A House of Singing

[16.] John Newton, 'How Sweet the Name of Jesus Sounds' (1779).

7. A House of Sympathy

[17.] Charles Dickens, *The Cricket on the Hearth* (Bradbury and Evans, 1845).

8. A House of Service

[18.] John Betjeman, *Archie and the Strict Baptists* (John Murray, 1977).

[19.] Smith, *You Are What You Love*.

[20.] The Daily Telegraph (25 November 2017).

10. A House of Sojourn

[21.] Dale Ralph Davis, *Focus on the Bible: Judges* (Christian Focus, 2015).

[22.] Patricia St John, *The Tanglewoods' Secret* (10Publishing, 2018).

23. Sandra McCracken, 'We Will Feast in the House of Zion' from *Psalms* (2015).

Conclusion: The Fruitful Home

24. David Prior, *The Message of Joel, Micah and Habakkuk* (IVP, 1998).

25. Rudyard Kipling, 'If' (1945).

26. J.R.R. Tolkein, *The Fellowship of the Ring, volume one of The Lord of the Rings* (Allen & Unwin, 1954).

10Publishing is the publishing house of **10ofThose**.
It is committed to producing quality Christian
resources that are biblical and accessible.

www.10ofthose.com is our online retail arm selling
thousands of quality books at discounted prices.

For information contact: **info@10ofthose.com**
or check out our website: **www.10ofthose.com**